ARE there Rainbows in SPACE?

PENGUIN WORKSHOP
An imprint of Penguin Random House LLC
1745 Broadway, New York, New York 10019

First published in the United Kingdom by Puffin Books, 2023

First published in the United States of America by Penguin Workshop,
an imprint of Penguin Random House LLC, 2025

Text copyright © 2023 by Dr. Sheila Kanani
Illustrations copyright © 2023 by Liz Kay

PENGUIN is a registered trademark and PENGUIN WORKSHOP
is a trademark of Penguin Books Ltd, and the W colophon
is a registered trademark of Penguin Random House LLC.

Visit us online at penguinrandomhouse.com.

Manufactured in China

ISBN 9780593889633   10 9 8 7 6 5 4 3 2 1 HH

Design by Emma Wells, Studio Nic&Lou

ARE there Rainbows in SPACE?

A COLORFUL Compendium of SERIOUSLY Cool SCIENCE

BY DR. SHEILA KANANI

illustrated by Liz Kay

PENGUIN WORKSHOP

To my rainbow family (J, B, V, and K),
who always remind me to count my
rainbows and not my storms!—SK

OUR COLORFUL WORLD

When you picked up this book, you may have been attracted to its bright colors or the rainbows on the cover. Can you name all the colors you can see? Which colors are most easily visible to humans? How does the natural world use color to help it survive?

You'll discover the answers to these questions—and many more—as you make your way through this book. We'll talk about light (the most important thing) and waves (not the kind you see at the beach—though you will learn why the sea looks blue!). You'll find out how some animals are able to glow in the dark and how others change their colors to hide from predators. You'll also discover why leaves change color in the autumn, why your veins look blue but your blood is red, and how the language we use shapes the colors we see.

And you'll learn exactly how to make a rainbow—in space.

So, first things first . . .

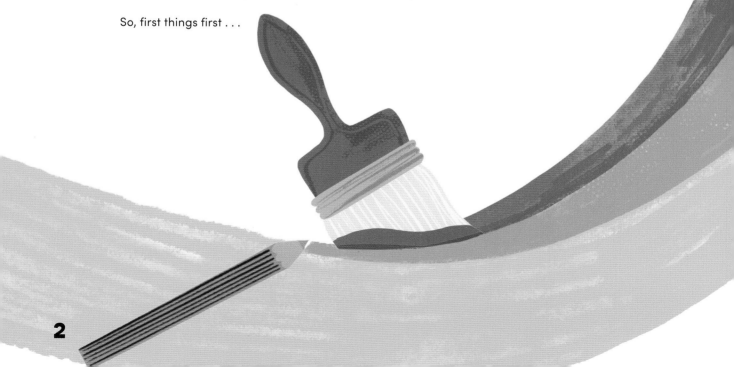

WHAT IS COLOR?

COLOR IS HOW WE SEE LIGHT

Light can come to us in two ways—direct or reflected. Direct light comes from something light-emitting, like a lamp or the Sun. Reflected light bounces direct light off the surface of something, like a table or a desk. Either way, our eyes pick up the light and enable us to see different colors.

VISIBLE LIGHT

The colors we can see come from visible light. This is any light that we humans are able to see with our eyes.

Humans can see three primary colors (red, green, and blue) and the rest of the color spectrum comes from mixtures of those three colors. You might be surprised to see green called a primary color, and not yellow—this is because green is a primary color for light. If you mix green and red when you're painting, you'll get a brown color—but when green and red light are mixed, they make the color yellow!

Visible light is part of a spectrum called the electromagnetic spectrum. Did you know that light is actually a type of energy? This energy is called electromagnetic radiation.

Apart from visible light, we can't see the majority of the electromagnetic spectrum with our eyes. Although we can't see them, machines that use the other energies that sit on the spectrum—like X-rays and microwaves—are part of our everyday lives. Can you think of any others?

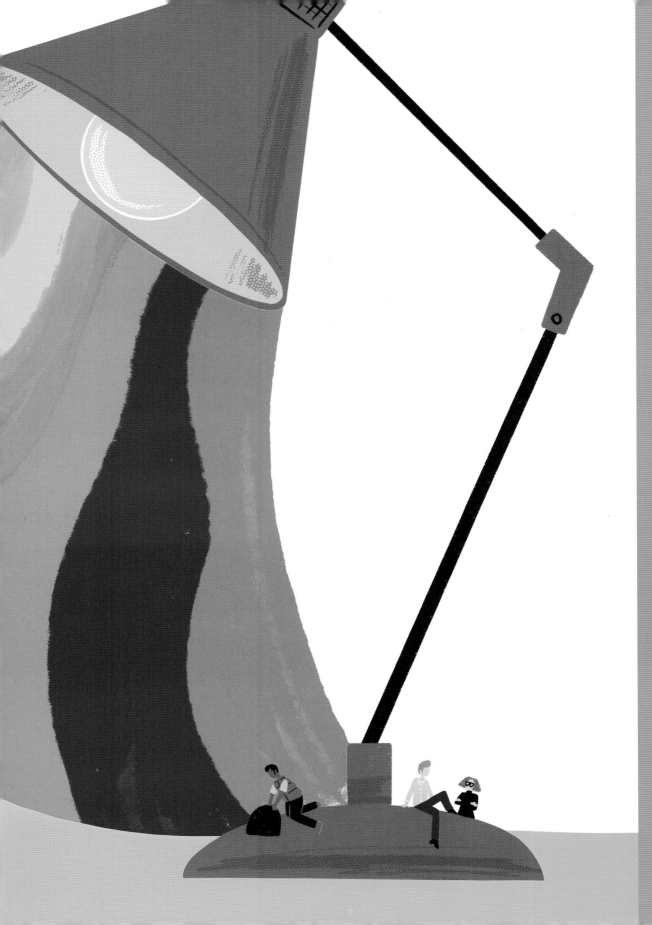

THE ELECTROMAGNETIC SPECTRUM CONTAINS MANY DIFFERENT TYPES OF LIGHT, INCLUDING:

- Gamma rays
- X-rays
- Ultraviolet light
- Visible light
- Infrared light
- Microwaves
- Radio waves

NO PINK?

The color we see as "pink" doesn't have a distinct wavelength in the way that the colors of the rainbow do. We see pink when our eyes register a mixture of red and blue light—which are at opposite ends of the visible spectrum.

LIGHT vs. VISIBLE LIGHT

Visible light and invisible light (like radio waves and X-rays—invisible to humans) are all electromagnetic waves. The only difference is that ultraviolet light, X-rays, and gamma rays all have shorter wavelengths than visible light. You can find out more about wavelengths on pages 7 and 92.

LIGHT FROM THE SUN

The visible light coming from the Sun is called "white light." This white light consists of red, orange, yellow, green, blue, indigo, and violet. You may know this list of colors by another name—a rainbow!

As white light is made up of all the colors of the rainbow added together, you can disperse white light using a prism to create a rainbow! In nature, raindrops act like prisms. The Sun's light shines through them, which is why we see rainbows when it rains.

This rainbow of colors is called the "visible spectrum." All the colors we know about can be made by mixing together the three primary colors: red, green, and blue. Our eyes can only detect the three primary colors—did you know that it's our brilliantly clever brain that mixes them together so we can see all the colors of the rainbow?

All colors have their own wavelength. It's a bit like a fingerprint for light!

WAVES

All light travels in waves. The distance from the top of one wave—the crest—to its next crest is called the wavelength. The shorter the wavelength, the more energy the light has. Violet light has a very short wavelength, so it has more energy than red light, which has a very long wavelength. As you can see, the colors of the rainbow are ordered from red, with the longest wavelength—the least energy—to violet, with the shortest wavelength—the most energy. Remember: all light has energy, and we have the ability to see light with the energy that corresponds to the primary colors.

But what about light with wavelengths longer than red, or shorter than violet? Those are the lights on the electromagnetic spectrum that are invisible to humans. Light with a longer wavelength than red is called infrared. Radio waves have the longest wavelength and the least energy. Ultraviolet light has an even shorter wavelength than violet light. And gamma rays have the shortest wavelength and most energy of all light!

HOW DO WE SEE COLOR?

OBJECTS REFLECT LIGHT

Have a look around! What can you see? A few things you spot might make their own direct light—a cell phone, a table lamp, the TV. These are known as luminous objects. However, most objects do not make their own light. These objects are nonluminous, and instead reflect the light given off by the luminous objects.

A IS FOR APPLE

From where I'm sitting, I can see a red apple. Light from the Sun outside is shining through my window, onto the apple. The apple is a nonluminous object, and so it absorbs some of the light—but some light bounces off it and into my eyes.

This reflected light enters the eye through the pupil (the opening in the middle). The light hits the back of the eye, the retina. On the retina, there are tiny cells that react to light. These are called rods and cones.

The job of the rods is to detect lightness and darkness, so they are most sensitive to black and white. The job of the cones is to detect bright light, or colors. The cones behave differently if they sense red, green, or blue light—the primary colors.

When the light from the red apple activates the cones, it sends an electrical signal to the brain along the nerves. When the brain gets the signal from the cones, it sends it back with a color—in this case, red!

If you add all colors of light together equally, you make white light for a white object. If you add none of the colors of light, the result is the absence of light: a black object.

Reflection is important, as it enables us to see nonluminous objects!

PAINTING WITH LIGHT

Apart from white and black, the way light mixes to make different colors is very different from the way colored paint is mixed, as we know from the difference between primary colors in your paintbox and primary colors for light. For example, when it comes to light, if you mix red and green, you get yellow. You can do some really clever color mixing with light if you know which colors to add or subtract.

COLOR BLINDNESS

Sometimes, parts of the eye may not work as we expect them to. This means some people don't see certain colors, or any colors at all. This is called color blindness. People with color blindness might not be able to tell the difference between certain colors. Some people are born with color blindness, or it can happen because parts of the eye, nerves, or brain become damaged during someone's life.

Some animals, like dogs and some species of monkeys, have evolved to be color-blind, so that they can detect things in dark or in low-light conditions more easily.

As we now know, humans can only see the visible light spectrum. We can't see other parts of the electromagnetic spectrum, like ultraviolet or infrared, unless we use special cameras or telescopes.

But did you know that some animals can see much more than the visible spectrum? Reindeer, birds, bees, and fish can see in ultraviolet, and snakes, frogs, and insects can see infrared! The natural world is full of astonishing facts, and you're about to discover a lot more of them.

So now we know how we see light, and therefore color. But what use does color have in the world we live in? Get ready to embark on a truly eye-opening journey through the universe, with a rainbow of visible light as our guide.

Evolution is the gradual changing and developing of a species over time.

SUPERVISION:
People with color blindness might be able to detect camouflage more effectively because of the way their color receptors work. While they might not be able to differentiate well between red, orange, and green, they could have extra sensitivity to other shades, like khaki.

THE COLOR RED

In China, red is the color of good luck and fortune, and has been used to color the gates and walls of royal palaces.

RED AT A GLANCE

Red is the color in the visible spectrum with the longest wavelength. It sits between infrared and orange, and can vary from pale pink to deep burgundy to bluey crimson.

Red is a primary color of light. Mix it with green light to get yellow light, or blue light to get magenta light.

INDIAN WEDDINGS

At Indian weddings, some brides wear a red sari, which symbolizes love, commitment, and strength.

Red was one of the very first colors used in prehistoric art. Paint was made from a naturally red-colored earth, called ochre. Ancient Egyptians used to cover their faces and bodies in ochre to celebrate victories, as did Native Americans—the Beothuk people of Newfoundland, one of the first tribes met by Europeans, used red ochre on their bodies as a sign of tribal identity.

Some Hindu women place red powder called *sindoor* along their hairlines, to show that they are married.

As red is the color of human blood, it has been linked to a warning of danger, and has also been used to symbolize war and victory.

During the European Renaissance (the fifteenth and sixteenth centuries), many people wore brilliant red clothes, dyed using crushed-up dried insects called cochineal. Plants such as madder can also be used to make red dyes, and are often less likely to fade than cochineal. Strong red dyes were expensive, so wearing red told everyone that you had enough money to buy red cloth.

THE COLOR OF LOVE?
All over the world, red is often the color people associate with love, passion, and romance!

WHY IS BLOOD RED?

Blood starts off bright red and full of oxygen. The heart pumps blood through the arteries to various places in your body.

BECAUSE OF HEMOGLOBIN!

This is a molecule that transports oxygen in the blood around the body. Hemoglobin has lots of iron in it, and it's this iron that gives blood its red color. Plus, the oxygen it carries makes that red color even richer.

WHY DO WE NEED THIS RED HEMOGLOBIN?

Humans need oxygen to fuel our organs. We breathe oxygen into our lungs, and it is absorbed into our bloodstream. Then it is carried around the body by the hemoglobin in our blood.

HEMOGLOBIN

DID YOU KNOW?

Adult humans have about five liters of blood in their body.

Some animals, like octopuses, do have blue blood! This is because copper, not iron, carries the oxygen in their blood and it makes it look blue, not red. There are even some animals with purple, clear, or green blood. (Imagine green blood coming out when you scrape your knee!)

Once the blood has delivered its oxygen, it picks up a waste product: carbon dioxide. Because the blood isn't full of oxygen anymore, it loses its brightness and becomes a dull red. The carbon dioxide is pumped by the heart back up to your lungs, and eventually you breathe the carbon dioxide out.

Imagine your arteries are like highways, and the hemoglobin in your blood is a car, carrying the oxygen from one place to another.

Sometimes people's veins look blue—you might notice this if you have pale skin around your wrists. But this is actually an optical illusion! Sunlight hits your skin and the red light is absorbed because of its long wavelength, which means it can travel through the skin and tissue easily, without being deflected or bouncing back. Blue light, with its short wavelengths and higher energy, is deflected more easily, and can't travel as deeply into the skin. The blue light is reflected back into your eyes, and thus your veins appear blue. (And the paler your skin is, the bluer your veins look.) But your blood is never really blue—it is always red, because of the hemoglobin, and only changes shade depending on how much oxygen is in it.

WHY is MARS KNOWN as the RED PLANET?

THE RED PLANET

Some people call Mars "the red planet" because of the red soil and rock that make up its surface. The rocks and soil contain the chemical element iron. Mars is also a very windy planet, which means there are often dust storms. The wind blows the iron all over the surface, and the oxygen within the wind causes the iron to rust—making the surface turn red.

DID YOU KNOW?

An atmosphere is a layer of gas that surrounds a planet. Earth's atmosphere is essential as it contains the air that plants and animals breathe to survive.

DID YOU KNOW?

Whenever anything made from iron reacts with oxygen, it turns rusty. Have you ever seen anything rusty—perhaps a rusty iron nail, or a rusty swing in a playground?

WHY DOES THE SKY ON MARS LOOK RED?

Light from the Sun shines through the atmosphere of Mars, just as it does on Earth, but the large amounts of rusty dust in Mars's atmosphere scatter the light. The dust particles are larger than the particles in our atmosphere, and these large particles absorb the blue light and scatter the red light, giving the sky its red tinge. Find out more about light scattering on page 75!

FLAMINGOS: YOU ARE WHAT YOU EAT

With their spindly legs and brilliant pink color, flamingos are fabulous birds. But did you know the reason they are pink is because they eat pink food?

Flamingos are born with whitish-gray feathers. These lovely birds live around lakes, so they eat algae, insect larvae like caterpillars and maggots, and soft-bodied creatures called mollusks and shrimps. These foods contain chemicals called pigments, and when flamingos eat a lot of them, the pigments cause the flamingos' feathers to turn from gray to pink! We find the same chemicals in tomatoes, sweet potatoes, carrots, and—surprisingly—spinach.

Flamingos across the world have slightly different shades of pink depending on where they live and what type of food is available. Caribbean flamingos are a brighter shade of orangey pink, while Kenyan flamingos are pale pink.

DID YOU KNOW THAT A BLACK FLAMINGO WAS ONCE SPOTTED?

Flamingo experts believe that its black color was caused by the bird having a lot of a pigment called melanin in its body, which turned its feathers very dark.

21

RED-BOTTOMED MONKEYS

Did you know that some monkeys have big red bottoms? There are many uses for a rear end like this!

The color red can show that the monkey is "in heat" (or ready to mate), and when it comes to size, a larger backside can be more comfortable to sit on. So female monkeys with big red bottoms are often seen as more attractive by male monkeys!

Female baboons have red bottoms. The color, shape, and size of their red backsides indicates to the male baboons that the females are ready to mate. For ten to twenty days each month, female baboons get swollen bottoms to show they are ready to start mating. When the skin is swollen, there is more red blood flowing through it, giving it that red color—and it's even more obvious because the baboons' bottoms don't have any fur!

These types of bottoms are known as ischial callosities. *Callosity* describes skin that has become thicker or harder over time. (You might notice a callous on your foot if it's been rubbed from doing lots of walking.) *Ischial* is a word describing the lower back and hip area.

Other monkeys have different color rears. Some have bright blue bottoms! The blue bottoms of some monkeys, like mandrills and lesulas, reflect blue light and absorb red light. Male mandrills have super colorful muzzles and bottoms, and these colors attract the female mandrills. The females think that the male mandrills with the brightly colored behinds are more physically strong, and it makes them want to mate with them. There is a bit of truth in this, as the male mandrills with the most testosterone shed the fur around their tail end, making their backsides stand out even more. Which color would you rather have?

The more colorful you are, the more important you are in your monkey family. So remember: a bright behind means you're the boss!

Testosterone is a hormone in many animals' bodies. The male of a species often produces the most testosterone.

WHY IS A HIPPO'S SWEAT RED?

Hippos live in very hot countries and have very sensitive skin. If they didn't wallow in mud and water all day, they would end up with dried-out, sunburnt skin. They spend their daytimes in water and go out to feed at nighttime to avoid the heat, but they have another built-in sun protection—red sweat!

When a hippo is hot, it produces a sticky, oily liquid from its skin that looks red in daylight. While human sweat works only to cool us down, the stuff that oozes out of hippos is actually a special ointment with loads of properties. It works as a sunscreen, repels water, moisturizes the skin, and can act as an antiseptic, too! It has been nicknamed "blood sweat" because of its red color, but it can actually change color in order to give the hippos as much protection against the Sun as possible. Sometimes it is clear, sometimes red, and sometimes orange! It is so effective that even albino hippos with very sensitive skin are safe under the midday sun.

Wouldn't it be supercool if humans had a natural sunscreen, antiseptic, and moisturizer built into our sweat?

HOW DOES SWEAT WORK?

Sweat is moisture that comes through the skin when a human or an animal is very hot or anxious. Sweat evaporates off the surface of the body, cooling down the temperature of the skin.

ORANGE

THE COLOR ORANGE

People used to create orange paint from a mineral called realgar. In ancient times this paint was used to decorate tombs, but it was very dangerous for humans, because realgar is a form of arsenic—a deadly poison.

ORANGE AT A GLANCE

Orange comes between red and yellow on the visible spectrum. This means it is a color with one of the longest wavelengths, and therefore some of the lowest energy, out of all the colors in the visible spectrum. Shades of orange include amber, peach, and coral.

When people see the color orange, they might think of fire, autumn, and sunsets—even though those things have plenty of other colors in them, too.

Just like red, orange signs can be used as a warning or a way to catch someone's attention, as it's an easy color for humans to see.

It is a special color to the religions Hinduism and Buddhism. In Hinduism, orange represents fire and purity.

WHAT CAME FIRST: ORANGE OR THE ORANGE?

The color orange was named after the fruit. Before that, it was simply called yellow-red! People used the word *orange* to describe the fruit two hundred years earlier than they used the word *orange* to describe the color.

In English, the word *orange*, comes from *pomme d'orenge*, the Old French word for the fruit, meaning "the fruit from the orange tree." That phrase derives from the Arabic word *naranj* and that word comes from the ancient Sanskrit *naranga*, which means "orange tree." Even today in Spanish, orange is *naranja*. As you can see, all these languages are related to each other.

Orange is worn by Blackpool FC, an English soccer team. Their nickname is "the Tangerines," for obvious reasons!

Saffron, a very fragrant (and expensive!) ingredient in cooking, has a golden orange color because it contains the chemical crocin. Saffron is the dried stigmas and styles of a type of crocus flower.

Orange is also the national color of the Netherlands.

29

THE ORIGINAL ORANGE

Did you know that oranges—and all citrus fruits—traditionally come from the borders of China, India, and Myanmar, way up in the Himalayas?

There are many different types of orange, from the red-colored blood orange to the popular, bright Jaffa variety. Ancient oranges were not sweet and were mostly used in medicines. The fruit we eat today—the sweet orange—is a cross between two ancient types of orange: the mandarin and the pomelo. Humans have been eating the sweet orange since at least 314 BCE—you can read about them in Chinese literature. Fossils of a leaf from a type of ancient orange tree were found in China, and dated back to eight million years ago!

Citrus fruits, including oranges, were spread across Asia by the Arab Empire, and eventually made it to Italy, then Spain. Christopher Columbus took orange seeds on his voyages, and by the 1500s Spanish adventurers had taken the fruit to Florida in what is now the United States.

YUM!
The best way to test the sweetness of an orange is to eat one . . .

FROM GREEN TO ORANGE

Orange trees are evergreen and, under the right conditions, can grow anywhere in the world. Traditionally they need quite warm weather, sunshine, and lots of water to grow lovely juicy oranges, but even these conditions can be replicated in countries with cooler climates, if you use equipment like a greenhouse or a conservatory. Orange trees are quite hardy—they can just about withstand freezing temperatures and snow (although the fruit from a cold tree won't be nearly as tasty).

In order for any tree to bear fruit, it needs to flower first. Orange flowers are small and white, and not all the flowers become oranges—most drop off the tree once they have finished flowering. Once the fruit has developed it can take up to a year and a half to mature into a ripe orange!

The best time of year to eat oranges is around Christmas, but the trees can make oranges at any time. And you don't always have to wait for the peel to turn orange before you eat it—navel oranges turn orange very quickly, but Valencia oranges can be sweet even if their peel is green!

FIRE AND FLAMES

When a fire burns, it can look orange. What is happening?
Why are the flames orange, and why are they hot? Well, it is
all about light, energy, and what substance is fueling the fire.

Fire burns because of combustion. This is a chemical reaction that takes
place between fuel and oxygen. The fuel can be a number of things, like gas
or wood. The fuel and oxygen are combined with the heat of friction (for
example, a match being struck), and the resulting combustion causes heat
and light to be given off. We feel the heat as it warms us, and we see the
light in the form of the flames.

The flame is hottest at its bottom, and coolest at its tip—though it is still
extremely hot throughout, so you wouldn't want to touch it! Even the coolest
flames are between 932°F and 1,832°F. You might notice that the hot base of
a flame is often white or blue, while the cooler top of the flame is yellow or
orange. Why is this?

COLOR AND TEMPERATURE

Different temperatures of fire give off different-colored light. Superhot fires
(which can burn at around 5,400°F) actually look blue all over, not yellow or
orange. In a wood fire (a fire in which wood is used as the fuel), the bright
color comes from the fact that wood contains carbon, an element that, when
it burns, gives off a yellow or orange color. But in a superhot fire, all the
carbon has been burned away and what's left is a cold blue-looking flame
(which is actually much hotter than the warm yellow flame).

Sometimes you might see flames with different colors from yellow, orange,
or blue, and these colors can come from burning different chemicals. Copper
burns green, for example, while a pink flame indicates the presence of the
chemical lithium chloride.

WHY ARE CARROTS ORANGE?

Well, a lot of them aren't! Although carrots are typically orange, these crunchy vegetables were originally a totally different color. Carrots started out white, but now you can also find purple, yellow, and red carrots. Carrots documented almost three thousand years ago in Central Asia were purple, and orange carrots weren't documented until many years later.

DOMESTICATION AND GENETIC MUTATION

Humans changed carrots to make them sweeter and tastier, and the colors were an accidental added extra! When humans intentionally change wild plants or animals, it is called domestication.

For hundreds of years, carrot seeds were used as medicine—people would eat the tops of the carrots (the leafy part) in the same way we now use herbs like parsley. At this time, the roots were thin and bland-tasting. Over time, the farmers used domestication to grow particular variations of carrot to get rid of the bitter taste.

As this domestication took place, the carrots began to grow in different colors. A genetic mutation occurred, which removed the purple pigment from the carrot and created a new variety: the yellow carrot. Genetic mutation is an unusual change in something's DNA—changing its very structure because an organism's DNA contains all the instructions it needs to develop, live, and reproduce.

Eventually, those once-thin roots evolved into a sweet and tasty crop, and people started eating the carrot root instead of the carrot top. Eventually, the orange carrot was developed through further farming.

Carrots are a root vegetable. This means the orange part— the part that we eat—is actually the root of the plant.

Orange is the national color of the Netherlands, and so Dutch carrot farmers began to grow orange carrots in the sixteenth century instead of the purple, white, and yellow ones. They intentionally grew more of the orange ones, which have higher beta-carotene levels (a naturally occurring plant pigment responsible for the orange color). Over time—and in part due to the work of nineteenth-century biologist Louis de Vilmorin, who dedicated his life to cultivating plants—orange carrots naturally became the most common variety.

THE GOOD KIND OF CHEMICALS

Beta-carotene turns into vitamin A in the human body. This vitamin aids your vision, helps your body fight illness and infection, and keeps your skin healthy. Different-colored carrots have different natural chemicals—for example, purple carrots have the red pigment anthocyanin in them. As well as making them look purple, it is also good for your heart.

DID YOU KNOW THAT IF YOU EAT TOO MANY CARROTS, YOUR SKIN COULD TURN ORANGE?

This is a condition called carotenemia, and the only way you can get your skin to turn back is by eating fewer carrots. But don't worry—you'd need to consume more than ten carrots every day for weeks in order for this to happen to you!

WHY do LEAVES TURN ORANGE in AUTUMN?

Don't you just love the seasons? The blossoms on the trees in the spring, the warm evenings in summer, and wrapping up warm and seeing snow fall in winter. But my favorite season has to be autumn, with those wonderful orange, red, and yellow leaves everywhere!

BUT WHY DON'T LEAVES JUST STAY GREEN?

Leaves look green because they contain something called chlorophyll, a green pigment found in plants. Plants need chlorophyll, sunshine, carbon dioxide, and water to make food, which normally takes the form of a sugary substance called sap. Chlorophyll absorbs energy from the Sun, and this turns the carbon dioxide and water into carbohydrates, like sugar and starch.

BUT DID YOU KNOW THAT LEAVES AREN'T REALLY GREEN?

Chlorophyll is so green that it hides the natural color of the leaves, and there is lots of chlorophyll in leaves during the spring and summer when plants are making the most of their food. But in the autumn and winter, when there is less sunlight (so less chlorophyll) and the temperature drops, the trees use less chlorophyll and produce less food. This means that the green color in the leaves fades away and the other colors of the leaves show up.

Underneath all the chlorophyll, leaves are naturally orange, yellow, red, and brown!

LEAVE NOW

In the autumn, many plants make less food and become weaker. The leaves fall from the trees because the weaker stems break, and eventually the trees become bare. This seems really bleak, but there are some benefits to a tree having no leaves! A tree without leaves can store moisture in its trunk and branches, which means it can survive a winter season without dying. And a tree without leaves is more protected during a winter storm, as the winds can blow through the bare branches without doing too much damage to the whole tree!

THE ORANGE OLM

Have you heard of the olm? It's an aquatic salamander in the amphibian family. Olms eat, sleep, and live underwater and are normally found in cave waters in Europe.

Aquatic describes something that lives in water, and an amphibian is a certain type of cold-blooded creature, like a frog, newt, or salamander, which can live in water and on land.

At first glance, olms look a bit like snakes or eels, and one of their nicknames is "baby dragons"—the frills around the olm's face do make it look a bit like a tiny dragon! They have long, thin bodies and a short tail with a fin on top.

LIVING IN THE DARK

Olms have lived in caves for millions of years, which means they have evolved and adapted to living in a dark, wet environment. They can't use their eyes to see in the dark, so over time they have evolved to be blind, but their other senses have become stronger to help the olms survive. Their hearing and their smell are almost like superpowers!

As the olm is a peachy orange color, another one of its nicknames is "human fish" on account of the "flesh color" of its skin. Of course, human flesh can be many different colors, but when the olm was given this nickname, "flesh color" referred to a stereotypical European flesh color (as olms are only found in certain caves in Europe). But, in fact, the olm's skin can be white, pink, or pale yellow. Because they live in dark caves, their skin has very little pigment and doesn't need much protection from sunlight. This means that their skin doesn't have a strong color. What we see as "orange skin" is blood showing through their thin, translucent skin! So olms aren't actually orange at all!

THE ULTIMATE COUCH POTATO

The life expectancy of an olm is up to one hundred years! Some olms can sit still for seven years at a time without the need for food, conserving their energy by not moving at all.

An olm's skin is so thin that sometimes you can see its insides from outside!

YELLOW

THE COLOR YELLOW

Yellow can be thought of as a happy, sunny color, but interestingly, in the Western world, it is many people's least favorite color.

YELLOW AT A GLANCE

Yellow comes between orange and green on the visible spectrum. Shades of yellow include gold, flaxen, mustard, and beige.

Yellow is a primary color for paint, but not for light. When it comes to light, you can make yellow by mixing red and green—but if you did this with paint, you'd make brown!

YELLOW CARD

In soccer, if you do something against the rules you may be given a yellow card for poor behavior.

The ancient Egyptians used yellow paint a lot because of its similarity to gold. They thought that the bones of gods were made from gold, and so yellow ochre was used in many tomb paintings. A yellow paintbox was even buried with King Tutankhamun.

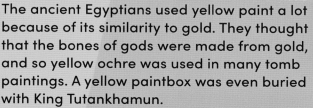

The color yellow appears on many world flags, including two of the countries with the highest populations in the whole world: China and Brazil.

Yellow paint has been around for thousands of years. There is a cave painting of a yellow horse in France that is believed to be seventeen thousand years old! Orpiment, a favorite yellow paint in ancient times, is a form of arsenic and very poisonous.

At a distance, yellow is the most visible color to the human eye. For this reason, it's used for high-visibility jackets, and as a warning color (just like red!).

Sometimes yellow is associated with cowardice—you might have heard the phrase "yellow-bellied." There are many theories about the origin of this phrase, but it might have come from the fact that people look a bit yellow when they are ill and weak, or it could have come from the fact that chickens can be yellow (if you call someone a chicken, you are also telling them that they are a coward!).

Even though yellow isn't everyone's favorite color, it appears in many famous songs, including "Yellow Submarine" by the Beatles, "Mellow Yellow" by Donovan, and "Yellow" by Coldplay. Can you think of any more?

Yellow is a very common color in nature, from flowers like daffodils and buttercups to food like bananas and lemons. There is a very famous painting of yellow sunflowers by the artist Vincent van Gogh. He loved the color yellow because it reminded him of sunshine and warm weather.

43

WARNINGS IN NATURE

Bees and wasps are quite distinctive because of their yellow-and-black-striped bodies. We will find out later that some animals are colored yellow to blend in with their surroundings and hide from predators (learn more about camouflage on page 56!). But wasps use their yellow-and-black stripes in a very different way.

The yellow color and the bold stripes are a warning sign for predators to leave them alone—or they will be stung. If you've ever been stung by a wasp, you will know how horrible it feels!

Some clever insects like hoverflies aren't dangerous, but do have yellow-and-black-striped bodies. Scientists think that hoverflies are copycats—they may have realized that if they look like wasps, predators avoid trying to eat them because they don't want to get stung. But hoverflies don't have stings—they just pretend to!

The most brightly colored wasps have the worst sting, while some wasps can't sting you at all. Those wasps often have no stripes and are brown in color.

THE GOLD STANDARD

Humans have been attracted to gold for thousands of years. But when you compare it to other metals, gold is not actually very special. It isn't useful because it is too soft, it doesn't react with other chemical elements, and while it does conduct electricity, it isn't magnetic. So why do humans love gold so much?

Gold is a bright yellow color, so it really catches the eye. But perhaps its most distinctive feature is its malleability. You can bash gold with a hammer until it is so thin that we call it "gold leaf." But being malleable can also be a bad thing—especially if you're looking for tough and strong metals. However, when it comes to gold, it is handy that we are able to make sheets and very thin wires of gold to use in electronics.

Gold leaf is edible, and chefs put it on their desserts and plates to make them look beautiful. Drinks sometimes have flecks of gold leaf in them, too, to give them a bit of sparkle! Some people think eating gold has health benefits like reducing swelling, but actually edible gold is more likely to just pass through your system without affecting your body. This means that the only benefit to eating or drinking things with gold in them is that you might have gold-flecked poop!

You can wear gold jewelry for many years without the gold going dull or losing its color because it doesn't react very easily with other elements. Gold jewelry was worn by the ancient Egyptians, and is still a favorite today.

MONEY, MONEY, MONEY

Gold's enduring popularity has seen it used to this day as currency to buy and sell things. The first gold coins we know of were made in Anatolia (now part of Turkey) in the sixth century BCE. Gold coins and gold bullion— bars of gold—are sometimes kept in secret banks by governments, to use as emergency money in times of war or hardship.

A RARE FIND

Gold is pretty rare on Earth. If you are going to use a metal for currency, you can't use something that you can find everywhere. If you did that, everyone could just dig it up and make their own money!

GOLD IN SPACE

Gold is an excellent electrical conductor, so very high-quality electronic equipment will have gold wires instead of the usual copper. Gold is highly reflective, too, and can be used to keep satellites in space at the right temperatures as well as to protect astronauts' vision, as gold is used in their helmet visors.

DID YOU KNOW?

In 95 BCE, a Chinese emperor, Hsiao Wu I, asked for a gold coin to be made to celebrate a special sighting of an animal he claimed to have seen—a unicorn!

47

IS THE SUN REALLY YELLOW?

What color would you use to color in the Sun? Maybe yellow—or red and orange? But if you were to measure the energy of the Sun from space, you would find it is green!

The Sun emits energy and light from all areas of the electromagnetic spectrum. It can give off X-rays, gamma rays, and visible light, and on the visible spectrum it can emit red, green, or violet light. If we look at the energy that the Sun gives off, it mostly emits energy at a wavelength around five hundred nanometers, which corresponds to a turquoise shade of green. But it doesn't look green! The color of the Sun alters depending on where you are on Earth, and in space.

SO WHY DOES THE SUN LOOK WHITE OR YELLOW?

The Sun emits all colors of visible light—red through blue—but its strongest is the green wavelength. And as you may remember, if you mix together all the colors of the rainbow, you make white light. This is the color of the light coming from the Sun (or any other star).

From our point of view on Earth, the Sun appears to change color because of the way that white light travels through our atmosphere. The Earth's atmosphere scatters away light at the blue and violet end of the spectrum. Colors with longer wavelengths (reds, oranges, and yellows) are not scattered away, so are visible to our eyes. On a sunny day, when the Sun is high in the sky, it might look yellow; at sunset, when it's down toward the horizon, it might look orange or red; and sometimes during dust storms the Sun can look pinkish. If you were an astronaut on the International Space Station and you looked at the Sun, it would appear white, because of the lack of an atmosphere.

On a really clear night, look up at the stars. Some will appear whitish, whereas others are visibly more blue-tinged. Now you know that the bluer ones are hotter!

THE COLOR SCALE FOR STARS

The color of the star depends on what temperature it is, what it is made from, and its size. The hotter and brighter and bigger a star is, the bluer it looks to us. Cooler, smaller stars look redder.

Our Sun currently sits in the "yellow" category, but in about five billion years, it will cool down and turn red.

A great place to start is the constellation Orion the Hunter. The top-left shoulder of Orion is the star called Betelgeuse. That star is an old, cool red star around 6,000°F. The bottom-right foot is called Rigel. That star is a young, hot blue-white star around 21,000°F.

GREEN

THE COLOR GREEN

Green is the official color of Islam, because it is associated with paradise.

GREEN AT A GLANCE

Green is the color in between orange and blue in the visible spectrum. It is in the middle in terms of energy and wavelength, midway between red and violet. Shades of green include mint, lime, emerald, jade, and sea green.

Green also represents safety. When it comes to traffic lights, whether you're a driver or a pedestrian, you know that green means you can safely go!

MONEY

Green has been known to represent wealth, which is why some countries, like the United States, have green-colored money.

Soldiers may wear green so that they can blend in with their surroundings. Many animals use camouflage, too.

THE UNITED STATES OF AMERICA
ONE DOLLAR

Green often makes people think of the Earth and nature. The word *green* comes from an Old English word, *grene*, which is a source of the words *grow* and *grass*—so even in the olden days, people thought of green as a color that represented nature and growth.

Green is a restful color to the eye, so if you are feeling tired, you should sit in a green room. This is partly the reason that hospitals use a lot of green on the walls and in the colors of their uniforms. The other reason doctors wear green scrubs is because green is the complementary color to red, so if doctors get red blood on them they will certainly be able to see it. A complementary color is one that is opposite a color on the color wheel.

Green appears on several flags. On the flag of India, it represents growth, and on the Irish flag, it represents the Catholic population. On Saint Patrick's Day, some cities dye their rivers green to celebrate!

GREEN-EYED MONSTER

If someone is called a "green-eyed monster," it means they are jealous. Linking being green-eyed to jealousy was first done by William Shakespeare in the seventeenth century!

Being called "green-thumbed" means you are good at gardening!

HUMANS and the COLOR GREEN

HUMANS CAN SEE MORE SHADES OF GREEN THAN ANY OTHER COLOR

We believe this is because our ancestors needed this ability so that they could see different creatures in nature. This is also the reason we use green vision for night-vision goggles—because our ability to see lots of shades of green means we can see many different objects and creatures through the goggles.

WHY ARE PLANT SHOOTS GREEN?

Most plants and trees have green shoots and leaves. This is because they all contain chlorophyll, a pigment that is important for plants to create food.

Chlorophyll makes plants look green because it absorbs red and blue light but reflects green light, which we see with our eyes.

Read more about chlorophyll on page 37.

RIPE AND READY

How do you know if a fruit is ready to eat? Do you squeeze it to see if it is soft? Do you smell it? Or maybe you make your decision based on its color? The same goes for animals that are trying to find ripe fruits to eat.

In nature, seeds are spread in order for the plant to reproduce itself—perhaps in other places, depending on where the seeds fall. This can happen by the fruit falling, being blown by the wind, or being eaten. Therefore, it is important that a fruit is eaten when its seeds are ready, so that the seeds pass through the animal and grow into a new plant. While its seeds are growing ripe, the plant tries to avoid being eaten, and this is when being a color that is off-putting to animals can come in handy. Many unripe fruits start off green (chlorophyll is to blame again here—there is a lot more green-light-reflecting chlorophyll in unripe fruits). Over time, the chlorophyll breaks down and other pigments are produced. For example, the pigment anthocyanin develops in strawberries, giving the fruit a different, more appetizing color.

Find out more about the color of fruits and vegetables on pages 30–31 and 34–35.

TIMING IS EVERYTHING

Did you know that green, red, orange, and yellow bell peppers are all the same fruit, just gathered at different times in their ripeness? Green peppers are the least ripe, which is why they can taste more bitter, and red peppers are the ripest, which is why they taste the sweetest. Which color peppers are your favorite?

WHY ARE FROGS GREEN?

Frogs might be the most well-known green animal on the planet. But why do they look green and how does this help them survive?

Frogs have many layers of skin, and the shade of green or brown of the frog depends on how light reflects through these layers. This helps a frog to hide in its surroundings, using camouflage to keep it safe from predators. A clever frog might look bright green on a leaf or in the grass, and then when it hops into a pond it might alter its color to a muddy green-brown, ensuring it stays hidden.

INVISIBILITY: A FROG'S SUPERPOWER

There are at least three layers of pigment in a frog's skin. The bottom layer looks dark brown, almost black. The middle layer reflects blue light from the Sun, and this reflected blue light travels through the yellowish top layer. When the yellow and blue light mix, we see a green frog! If a frog didn't have the top layer of pigment, it would look bright blue.

By adjusting how much light is reflected through its skin layers, the frog can change its color, protecting it from predators. Imagine if humans could change the color of their skin in order to hide more effectively—it would make for a great game of hide-and-seek!

There are many animals that are able to change color, including squid, chameleons, octopuses, and cuttlefish. These creatures can change color really quickly by changing the structures of the layers in their skin. They send lightning-fast signals between their brain and their skin cells. The brain tells the skin cells to stretch and squash, and when the cells expand, their colors look brighter. Octopuses are one of the most intelligent creatures on the planet, and they can even change the texture of their skin to match coral, rocks, and shells and hide from predators.

MOOD SWINGS

Chameleons don't change color to hide from predators— we now think that they change color to show off how they're feeling! In a similar process to frogs, chameleon skin has layers in it, and these layers reflect light in different ways in order to change color. Chameleons even change the structure of their skin to change their color dramatically, and this happens when a chameleon's mood changes. Excited chameleons reflect more red, orange, and yellow light, so appear to be those colors, and relaxed chameleons reflect light at the other end of the spectrum, so appear to be blue or purple! What if your skin changed color depending on how you were feeling?

close-up of a frog's skin

57

IS GREEN THE SAME IN EVERY LANGUAGE?

Did you know that the colors you see might depend on what language you speak? Every single human "sees" color in a slightly different way, and some can't see different colors at all. It's down to how our eyes work and the sensitivity of the cones in our retinas.

But it isn't just about the science of color—how you experience color can also be affected by the language you speak.

Many of the languages spoken across the globe didn't start out with different words for "green" and "blue." Instead they treated both colors as different shades of the same hue and called the color the equivalent of "grue." This is true for many people, from the Himba people in Namibia, to the Berinmo in Papua New Guinea, to the Welsh, Japanese, and Chinese. Over time, many of these cultures have taken "grue" to mean blue, and have created a new word to mean green.

People who speak Vietnamese and Zulu still use the same words for green and blue. They might say phrases like "blue like the sky" or "green like the leaves" to show the difference between what they mean.

Some languages, like Greek and Turkish, have different words for light blue and dark blue and green. This means that Greek and Turkish people are more aware of different shades of green and blue.

Some people can "hear" color and "see" sound because of particular connections between their senses—this is called synesthesia.

Interestingly, the more words a language has for different colors, the more colors the person who speaks that language can see. People who have many different words for "green" will be accustomed to looking at different shades of similar greens, whereas people who have fewer words for green may struggle.

Across the world there are six main ways for naming green and blue.

1. Two separate words for "green" and "blue"

2. The word equivalent to "grue," used for both blue and green

3. One word to represent green–blue–black

4. One word for blue–black and one word for green

5. The use of *green* to include all greens, from yellowy green to bluey green

6. One word for blue and one word for yellow–green

LIGHTS IN THE SKY

The Earth is home to two amazing natural light shows—the northern lights, or aurora borealis, and the southern lights, or aurora australis. Both create curtains of light that move across the sky in ripples of green, blue, pink, and purple.

The northern and southern lights are visible to the naked eye, so humans have witnessed them for many years. But if you have a good camera or other equipment, you can take incredible photos of them.

BEHIND THE CURTAIN OF LIGHT

The aurora borealis and aurora australis show us exactly what happens when energy from the Sun meets our atmosphere on Earth. The Sun is incredibly active, releasing energy particles into space all the time. This is called a "solar wind." The solar wind blows from the Sun all the way to Pluto and farther, interacting with the planets along the way.

Meanwhile, the Earth has a magnetic field which acts like a force field, protecting us from the solar wind.

But at the North and South Poles, there are places where the solar wind does funnel down into the Earth's atmosphere. The energetic particles from the Sun smash into the particles in our atmosphere, heating up the gas particles in our air and making them glow. We see this glowing as the wonderful aurora.

The aurora borealis can be seen in places near the North Pole, such as Norway, Sweden, and Iceland. The aurora australis can be seen in places near the South Pole, including Australia and New Zealand.

DID YOU KNOW?
Spacecraft have observed auroras on other planets—Jupiter, Saturn, and even Mars have been seen to have auroras.

If the solar wind got down to the surface of the Earth, it would cause all sorts of havoc—for example, it could damage satellites or affect GPS systems.

Different gases in the atmosphere glow different colors: a green aurora shows us where oxygen is, and a purple-blue aurora shows us where nitrogen can be found.

BLUE

THE COLOR BLUE

In Greece, you might find a glass charm in the shape of a blue eye. This is said to ward off evil spirits.

BLUE AT A GLANCE

Blue is one of the three primary colors of light, and can be found at the more energetic end of the visible spectrum, in between green and indigo. Shades of blue include cyan, cobalt, sky, azure, and navy.

Blue paint used to come from crushing a precious stone called lapis lazuli, so blue was very expensive. This meant that artists only used blue to paint very important things.

Blue is quite an important color for humans, because we see it so much in nature. It is often said to be the most popular color among people, and it has been important in art and decoration since ancient Egyptian times.

FEELING BLUE

Often we say something is blue, like blueberries, when it is actually purple (closer to violet on the color spectrum). And the blue whale is actually more of a grayish color!

There isn't much food that is naturally blue, and our brains might think of mold when we see it, so humans tend to avoid blue-colored food.

The Hindu god Lord Krishna has blue skin, which is said to be because he drank poisoned milk when he was a baby.

FEELING BLUE

How does the color blue make you feel? I love blue, because it makes me think of the sea, so I feel calm and happy. Other people find blue a cold color that might make them feel sad. But if you started to look blue—with a blue tinge to your skin—it could mean that your blood isn't pumping oxygen to your body properly, so you'd better get to the doctor!

WHY IS THE SEA BLUE?

When you fill a glass with water, what color is your drink? Clear, right? So why does seawater look blue?

The water absorbs the longer wavelengths of light—red, yellow, orange—and the scattered blue light is reflected. When the blue light enters our eyes, we see a blue sea.

If the seawater is very deep, or full of particles such as mud, algae, or silt, the scattered light might alter the color of the water, so that we see water in different shades of blue or greeny-brown. When the sea is very deep, even more colors are absorbed, and that part of the sea appears an even darker blue.

Another reason for the sea's color is the tiny algae that live there. These algae, known as phytoplankton, have lots of green chlorophyll in them. The chlorophyll reflects green light, giving the sea a green-blue tinge.

TURNING OF THE TIDE

Did you know that sometimes the tide can turn red? This is because of a particular type of algae that blooms like a flower. The algae blooms can be dangerous to marine life, though, because they release toxic substances into the water. A red tide along the northeast coast of England in 1968 caused the death of many seabirds.

DID YOU KNOW?

The Red Sea isn't actually red in color. The origin of its name is unknown, but it could either come from red algae found in the Red Sea, or because of one translation of "red" that also means "south."

CLEAR VISION

Blue eyes are surprisingly rare: only 10 percent of the world's population are said to have them. And did you know that blue eyes are another optical illusion?

The color in your eyes comes from the pigment in your iris, and also depends on how light is reflected around the cloudy fluid in the top layer of the iris. People with blue eyes have no pigment at all—so really, we should call them clear eyes!

In human eyes, the iris can contain pigments in colors from light brown to black. People with brown eyes have large amounts of pigment in their iris. The pigment absorbs a great deal of light, giving them dark eyes.

If you have green, blue, or hazel eyes, you have much less pigment, and your eyes look that color because of the way the light is scattered through the iris, in an optical illusion called structural colorization. As people with blue eyes have no pigment in their iris, it means that blue light isn't absorbed into their eyes. Instead it is reflected back out, making it appear that the person has blue eyes.

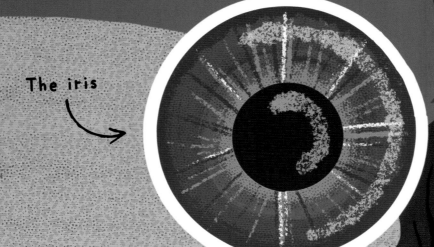

The iris

THE EYES OF HISTORY

Even more interesting is where blue eyes came from. Brown eyes used to be the default eye color for humans, but some time about six thousand to ten thousand years ago there was a genetic mutation, which caused clear eyes— what we know as blue. That means everyone with blue eyes can be linked back to a single person who lived many thousands of years ago!

Eye color is passed down from generation to generation. But working out what color eyes you might have isn't as simple as looking at the eye color of your parents. Having blue eyes is something known as a recessive trait and can depend on a few factors, meaning that just because both your parents have blue eyes, it won't necessarily mean you will, too.

DID YOU KNOW?

Most babies are born with blue eyes. The dark-colored pigment in the iris develops over time, so many newborn babies have blue-looking eyes to start with.

ONCE IN A BLUE MOON

You might have heard the phrase "once in a blue moon" used to refer to something that happens rarely. But in reality, a blue moon isn't actually when our moon turns blue—a blue moon describes a time when we get two full moons in one month, which happens about once every two or three years.

It would be amazing if the Moon did actually turn blue on a blue moon, but that sadly isn't the case! The only time the Moon appears to change color is during a lunar eclipse—when Earth's shadow blocks the Sun's light, and the Moon looks red—or if something unusual happens in our atmosphere, like a volcanic eruption, which could cause the Moon to appear a different color because dust in the atmosphere affects the reflected light.

Some Native American tribes have names for all the full moons in the year. The names for each moon are different between (and sometimes among) Native tribes. For example, for the Ojibwe tribe, some moon names include the Great Spirit Moon in January, the Bear Moon in February, the Snow Crust Moon in March, the Broken Snowshoe Moon in April, and the Blooming Moon in June. You might also have heard of the "harvest moon," which is the first full moon after September 21— the autumnal equinox.

DID YOU KNOW?

There is a record of a "real" blue moon, seen on December 10, 1883, caused by freak atmospheric conditions following a volcanic eruption, which made it appear blue.

MOON PHASES

The phases of the Moon are caused by the fact that the Moon goes around the Earth and the Earth goes around the Sun. At different times during its orbit, the Moon is either being lit up by the Sun, or is in shadow.

If the Moon, the Earth, and the Sun are all aligned, the Sun will light up an entire side of the Moon, and from Earth we see that as a full moon in the sky.

There are eight moon phases. The first is the new moon, when the Moon is completely in shadow and we can't see it. Then it waxes—it appears to increase in size from waxing crescent, then first quarter, then waxing gibbous, until we see a full moon. Once this is reached, the Moon wanes—appears to get smaller again—from waning gibbous, to last quarter, then waning crescent, to new moon, when it isn't visible. Then the whole cycle starts again.

The Moon takes about twenty-nine and a half days to complete all its phases and orbit all the way around the Earth, which means the moon phases (new moon→full moon→new moon again) takes 354 days to do twelve cycles. We have twelve months per year, so we would normally see twelve full moons each year. But there are 365 days in a normal year, not 354, so we see an extra full moon approximately every two and a half years. This thirteenth full moon in a year is called the blue moon.

DID YOU KNOW?

The word month comes from the Old English word monath, which in turn comes from a Germanic word for moon.

WHY is THE SKY BLUE?

You might think that the sky is blue because it reflects the color of the ocean, but that isn't the case. The sky looks blue no matter where you are—even if you are miles away from the sea!

BLUE LIGHT

Blue light travels in shorter, smaller waves than other colors, which causes it to scatter more.

RAYLEIGH SCATTERING

The sky is blue because of how sunlight interacts with our atmosphere. We already know that sunlight is made up of all the colors of the rainbow. When sunlight travels through our atmosphere, the molecules in the air cause the blue light to scatter the most and the red light to scatter the least, giving the sky its blue color. This scattering is called Rayleigh scattering, after the nineteenth-century British physicist Lord Rayleigh.

Sometimes the sky appears pinkish red—such as at sunset. This is also due to Rayleigh scattering. The Sun is lower in the sky, and this means the light has a thicker atmosphere to travel through. More blue light is scattered—to the extent that it gets scattered away—but the red light remains, so the sky gives us a pretty red sunset.

HIGH IN THE SKY

The air that is highest in the sky is the thinnest. The air closest to the Earth's surface has more weight because it is compressed by all the other air above it.

INDIGO &
VIOLET

THE COLORS
INDIGO and
VIOLET

Purple colors are actually mixtures of violet light with other-colored light, like blue or red. Shades of purple include mauve, lavender, lilac, amethyst, and fuchsia.

INDIGO AND VIOLET AT A GLANCE

Indigo is found between blue and violet on the visible color spectrum, traveling in small, short waves. Violet sits at the highest-energy end of the visible spectrum, after indigo. After violet, the light waves become even shorter. Their wavelength increases, and we leave the visible spectrum and move into ultraviolet, which humans can't see.

Purple has been associated with people in positions of authority, like royalty, judges, emperors, and religious leaders.

If someone has porphyrophobia, they are afraid of the color purple.

To make purple paint, artists have to mix red and blue pigments. There are cave drawings in France that can be dated back more than twenty thousand years that feature purple made by mixing the minerals hematite and manganese. Later, artists mixed red and blue pigments to make the shade they wanted.

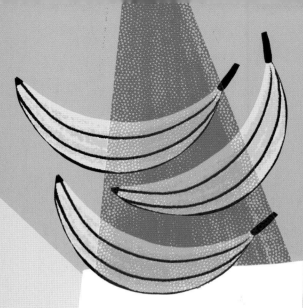

A RIPE GLOW

Did you know that overripe bananas glow indigo under ultraviolet light? The reason the banana starts to glow is because of a chemical reaction that happens when the chlorophyll breaks down. Because some insects and birds can see in ultraviolet, they can tell that the fruit is ripe, even in the dark.

In the early 1900s, purple was one of the colors representing the women's suffrage movement. It represented the instinct for freedom and dignity that flowed in their blood.

There's a myth that the word *purple* doesn't rhyme with anything. In fact, it does have rhymes: *curple*, which means the backside of a horse, and *hirple*, a word from Scotland that means "to hobble"!

Purple features frequently in the natural world, from purple frogs to purple broccoli, artichokes, lilac plants, grapes, eggplants, herons, and fish.

INDI-COME, INDI-GO

People all over the world wear blue jeans, but it is actually indigo dye that is used to color the denim cloth. Blue jeans were first created to be worn as workwear for farmers and miners in America. Then, in the 1950s, many famous actors in Hollywood began to wear them, which made them more popular—and the rest is history.

Denim fades and shapes to the body as it is worn, and many people like that, as it makes the jeans more personal and reflects the adventures that have been had in them.

Because the indigo dye fades when washed, some people don't wash their jeans very often at all. In fact, a microbiology student conducted an experiment and didn't wash a pair of jeans for a year and a half, and found that there was almost no change in how much bacteria was in them. So next time someone tells you to wash your jeans, you can tell them that you don't need to!

Jeans are made from a cotton cloth called denim, first made at Nîmes in France. The cloth was called *serge de Nîmes*, which became denim.

INDIGO DYE

Indigo dye is extracted from a variety of plants—many from the family known as *Indigofera*, which grow in the tropics, especially India. The plants that make the dye have been an important commercial crop for hundreds of years. Natural indigo dye fades when exposed to sunlight or washing, but today, chemical dyes that do not fade are mostly used.

Isaac Newton used the word *indigo* to describe the new color he found when studying the rainbow in 1675.

Tyrian purple dye smelled dreadful. The smell could get into the cloth that was dyed, too!

TYRIAN PURPLE

In ancient times, as long as 3,500 years ago, purple dye was created by crushing tiny murex sea snails. The dye was made by removing the snails from their shells, drying them, removing the juice from a gland, boiling the juice, then putting the liquid in sunlight. The juice turned white, then green, and finally violet. To get the right shade, the juice had to be removed from the sunshine at the exact time it reached the desired shade of purple.

This deep purple was called Tyrian purple, as it came from the ancient city of Tyre in Phoenicia (today, Tyre is in Lebanon). Clothes that were dyed Tyrian purple were luxuries, and very expensive. Until recently, you could visit the site and see mountains of shells left over from creating the dye. Sadly, the snails have been driven to extinction and can't be found in Lebanon anymore.

Tyrian purple dye can be re-created, but still costs enormous amounts of money. Less than one ounce of Tyrian purple dye can cost over three thousand dollars!

CORAL

You may have seen photos of coral reefs, or maybe you've been lucky enough to swim through one. Pictures often show incredible rainbow hues of coral forests, but what is coral? And why is it so colorful?

In shallow ocean waters, you might be able to see masses of beautiful purple-colored coral. Purple coral is colored by purple algae, which change color depending on how much light shines on them—a bit like coral sunscreen! The more sunlight that shines on those parts of the coral, the more purple sunscreen pigment is created. This protects the coral from ultraviolet light from the Sun, which can be harmful and cause coral bleaching. As you get deeper, the color fades, as most of the light has been absorbed by the water.

Coral is actually a living creature, not a plant or a rock, even though it might look like it. Reefs are made up of individual corals, which are animals with exoskeletons made from the chemical compound calcium carbonate.

Coral reefs are found in all the oceans on Earth, from the freezing-cold waters of the Antarctic to the tropical waters of the Indian Ocean. Coral comes in all sorts of colors: green, brown, pink, purple, red, yellow, and blue. The color comes from algae that live in the coral, and depends on the different amounts of algae within it.

SAVE OUR SEAS

Sadly, we also see white coral these days. This happens if the algae that live in the coral have died. The algae are really sensitive and can be killed by too much sunlight, temperature changes, stress, pollution from humans, and very low tides. This process of algae dying is called coral bleaching. Without its main food source, the coral is very vulnerable; its growth may become stunted, and it may become more susceptible to disease. Many other creatures depend on the coral reef for their own survival, so the bleaching of the coral reefs can have a very damaging effect on the environment.

An exoskeleton is a skeleton on the outside of a creature's body.

DID YOU KNOW?
Coral is completely unique—its color is different from one type to another. Even two corals sitting next to

IRIDESCENCE IN NATURE

A NATURAL RAINBOW

Iridescence is when you can see a rainbow of colors in one object—you might have seen this happen when you blow bubbles in soap. The greeny, bluey, purply color of iridescent insects and animals is beautiful to look at, but how does iridescence work?

Iridescent animals appear to change color depending on the angle from which you look at them. Iridescence isn't because of a purple pigment in the animal's skin, but is instead due to the structure of the skin and how light is affected by it.

There is a specific way that light hits feathers, wings, or scales, and returns to our eyes: when the light hits, it passes through many layers. In each layer, some of the light is reflected, and some passes down into the next layer. This can make the colors we see stronger or weaker, and the colors can also change depending on the distance between the layers and from which direction we are looking.

Find out more about camouflage on page 56!

Some iridescent animals—like Indian purple emperor butterflies—use this superpower as camouflage.

The fact that iridescent animals appear to sparkle or shine can be off-putting for predators. They might think the shiny butterfly is actually a sparkling drop of water or a shiny leaf, instead of food.

Iridescent animals can also use their shininess to stun predators with their colors, giving them a few seconds to escape!

The amount of iridescence depends on how you look at the butterfly—from one angle it may appear a shiny purple, and from the opposite angle it might just look black and white.

YOU'RE TURNING VIOLET, VIOLET!

Maybe you've heard the rhyme "Roses are red, violets are blue" . . . but violets aren't really blue—they're violet, of course.

A huge amount of natural science goes into coloring flowers. Violet flowers contain the pigment anthocyanin, which gives red, purple, and blue plants their rich coloring.

The brighter a flower is in color, the more likely it is to attract birds and bees to pollinate it. Birds and insects notice the bright colors and land on the flower. When they fly away, they take pollen with them—stuck either on their feet or in their furry bodies—and the pollen is naturally spread around to make more flowers.

Like many other flowers, violets are sensitive and can change color depending on their environment, such as how much food and light they get, and what sort of soil they are in. Violets can grow in hidden corners of the garden, quite low down.

In Britain, wild violets like to grow in damp but well-drained soil. They enjoy light shade and some sunshine. If you tried growing violets in other conditions, you might end up with white flowers instead of purple ones.

Remember beta-carotene (the pigment that makes carrots orange) and chlorophyll (the pigment that makes leaves green)? It's the same chemical process as this!

Have you heard the phrase "shrinking violent"? It comes from the fact that violets grow near the ground, and can be hard to find. They seem like shy plants!

PEACOCKS: AN OPTICAL ILLUSION

Did you know that peacocks' feathers aren't actually purple? They are really colored brown. It's science that makes the feathers appear purple, turquoise, green, and teal.

It is all to do with the structure of a peacock feather. If you look at one under a microscope, you can see grooves, lumps, bumps, and dips on it. Any light shining on peacock feathers bounces around because of these grooves, and all the different light waves interfere with each other. This causes the human eye to see all the wonderful colors.

Next time you see a peacock, you can surprise people by telling them that even though peacocks look like they have a rainbow of colors in their feathers, they are actually completely brown!

This structural colorization also happens to butterflies and ducks.

WINGING IT

Some animals appear shinier to attract a mate. Male mallards have iridescent green-purple heads—this is to make them more attractive and beautiful to the opposite sex. Female mallards have iridescent patches under their wings that can only be seen properly when they are flying. We believe the reason they have these streaks is so that they can attract the attention of other ducks during flight.

BIRDS OF A FEATHER

We often don't think very highly of the common pigeon, but they also have iridescent purple feathers around their necks. Male pigeons tend to have more of these shiny feathers, which sparkle between green and purple hues. It is believed that pigeons can see in ultraviolet light, and these purple neck feathers might "glow" in the dark. If this is true, then pigeons might be able to use their iridescent necks to communicate with each other in ways that are invisible to humans.

Find out more about ultraviolet light on page 92.

BRIGHT DIRECTION

The word *iridescence* comes from the Greek *iris*, which means "rainbow." Iridescence can also happen in clouds, when there are large numbers of raindrops or ice crystals in the cloud, which scatters the light from the Sun. Iridescent clouds are rainbow-tinged, which is cool—but pretty rare!

STARLINGS

Starlings also have iridescent feathers. There are many types of starlings across the globe, and even the common starling has some iridescence. Scientists think that the shininess of these birds may have helped them become widespread across the world. This is because their colors—and the fact that they use them to attract a mate—have made them more evolvable.

Starlings are iridescent because of the structure of their feathers. Starlings change color depending on how many layers of feathers they have, which alters how much light can shine and reflect through. They use their iridescence to communicate with other starlings, and their shiny feathers also help them deter predators.

Starlings fly to roost in huge flocks, called murmurations. The murmurations appear to flash, depending on which direction the birds are flying in. This can confuse predators enough to make them fly away, meaning that the flock of starlings is safe to live another day.

Healthier starlings are more iridescent, so if you see a brightly colored starling, you know it's well-fed and happy. This is also true of the brilliantly iridescent *Chrysilla volupe* jumping spider.

Just look at those colors!

BEYOND THE Rainbow

We've learned a lot about the visible color spectrum, but what about the rest of the electromagnetic spectrum—the parts that are invisible to the human eye?

INFRARED AND ULTRAVIOLET

Infrared light (IR) is below the color red in the electromagnetic spectrum. *Infra* means "below."

This means it has a longer wavelength and less energy than red light. In fact, the wavelength of IR is so long, humans can't see it with their naked eyes. However, we can image—that is, create a representation of—objects in IR using special cameras and computers. Humans can also sense IR as heat, and we use it in a great number of everyday things—from toasters to TV remote controls.

Infrared telescopes see the universe in IR instead of visible light. This gives us information about the heat energy given off by objects in space. Everything in the universe has heat energy—even if it's just a teeny, tiny amount.

Some things give off a whole lot of infrared—like a fire, or the Sun!

Ultraviolet (UV) is also part of the electromagnetic spectrum. *Ultra* means "in excess of," or "beyond," so it describes how UV is beyond violet in the electromagnetic spectrum.

This means it has a shorter wavelength and more energy than violet light. Human eyes can't see such short wavelengths, so we can't see UV light without additional technology.

UV has more energy than visible light, and this means it can be dangerous to us. UV light comes from the Sun. Over time, humans living in cool countries—which get less UV light from the Sun—adapted to have lighter skin.

Humans can use UV properties in science and technology. A UV lamp giving off ultraviolet light can be used to kill germs and sterilize kitchens. White clothes also seem to glow in the dark when a UV lamp shines on them!

The dark pigment melanin in human skin absorbs UV rays, which protects it from sunburn.

THE ELECTROMAGNETIC SPECTRUM

Increasing energy ⟶

Radio waves   Microwaves   Infrared   Visible light   Ultraviolet   X-rays   Gamma rays

⟵ Increasing wavelength

ANIMAL SIGHT BEYOND THE VISIBLE SPECTRUM

Humans can generally see more colors than animals, but our eyes are limited to the visible spectrum. Animals don't always see all the colors of the visible spectrum, but some can see in IR and UV, which humans can't.

Some snakes, like pit vipers and rattlesnakes, can see in infrared—this means that they can see heat. Pit vipers have something called a "pit organ," which helps their eyes to see infrared wavelengths. Pythons see infrared using little dips near their mouths to detect the light. Snakes have evolved to be able to see infrared because it helps them hunt. They are cold-blooded, but they eat warm-blooded animals like mice and birds. As the snakes can see infrared— meaning they see the heat given off by the warm-blooded animals—it is easier for them to hunt and find food in the dark.

Reindeer, rats, spiders, and insects can see in ultraviolet. Bees use their ability to see UV light to find flowers and nectar. Flowers often reflect UV light, so bees can spot them no matter the weather.

NATURE'S LIGHT

Have you heard of fluorescence? What about luminescence, phosphorescence, or bioluminescence?

Nature has an amazing way of making and using light for lots of incredible things. In the next few pages, we'll take a look at everything from luminous body paint to fish that can glow in the dark and bugs that create their own light.

INCANDESCENCE

If an object is incandescent, it gives off light because it is very hot. Examples include incandescent light bulbs, lava, and stars.

LUMINESCENCE

This describes light from a not-heated object, so it is the opposite of incandescence. If you touch a luminescent object, it won't necessarily feel hot.

PHOTOLUMINESCENCE

This is a particular type of luminescence. Specifically, it is when an object gives off light after getting energy from a different form of light energy (for example, anything in the electromagnetic spectrum). The object absorbs the energy at a certain wavelength and then emits it at a different wavelength (usually a longer one).

BIOLUMINESCENCE

Bioluminescence describes light that comes from a living thing. Some creatures can produce their own light using chemical reactions inside their bodies—they don't need a source of energy (like the Sun) to give off light.

You can find out more about the different types of luminescence and photoluminescence on pages 98–100.

A BIOLUMINESCENT FLY

Fireflies mix oxygen and other chemicals inside their bodies to create light. It is important that this chemical reaction is a type of luminescence (rather than incandescence) because it means that the firefly can light up without getting too hot and burning itself. Fireflies light up for several reasons. Firefly larvae—sometimes called glowworms—glow to tell predators that they'll taste bad, and adult fireflies use their light to attract other fireflies so that they can mate. Firefly squid work in a similar way, and communicate with other squid by making different parts of their bodies flash and light up to create patterns of light signals. They also use the flashing patterns to act as a way of putting off or deterring predators.

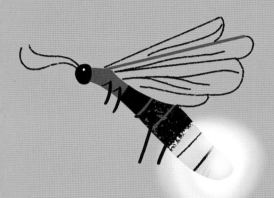

BIOLUMINESCENT SEA CUCUMBERS

Some sea cucumbers are bioluminescent. Did you know that sea cucumbers can detach pieces of their body? This is really clever as it means that if they are under attack, a glowing piece of the cucumber can break off and distract the predator, while the sea cucumber crawls away.

BIOLUMINESCENT ALGAE

Bioluminescent algae glow when their environment changes. For example, if the algae float from a very salty part of the ocean to a less salty part of the ocean, they may glow. Or if a human wades in a sea where there is bioluminescent algae, the person's feet might disturb the algae, causing them to glow. One type of bioluminescent algae is called *Noctiluca*, or "sea sparkle."

BIOLUMINESCENT FISH

The most famous bioluminescent fish is the angler fish. It has a filament coming out of the top of its head, like a fishing rod. At the end of the filament there is a ball, and the angler fish can light this ball up whenever it wants—usually to attract its prey. Angler fish live deep in the ocean where it is very dark, so when smaller fish see the glowing ball in the darkness, they become curious. The smaller fish swim over to the ball, then SNAP! The angler fish gobbles them up in its massive jaws.

FLUORESCENCE

A FORM OF PHOTOLUMINESCENCE

If something is fluorescent, it can produce its own light, and it does this by absorbing other types of light or energy (photoluminescence). Specifically, it is the ability to absorb short wavelength light and give off longer wavelength light. For example, in many parts of the world, paper money has a fluorescent security thread on it. If you put the money under a UV lamp, the security thread absorbs the UV light and gives off visible light. If this happens, you know the money is real. As soon as you take the UV light away, the paper money stops emitting visible light.

PHOSPHORESCENCE

This is a type of fluorescence (and therefore photoluminescence), but objects that are phosphorescent can give off light even after their energy source has been switched off or goes away. Phosphorescent objects can glow for seconds, or even hours, after their energy source has disappeared.

Glow-in-the-dark paint can be fluorescent or phosphorescent. Some glow-in-the-dark paint has phosphors in it, which are special chemicals that can be made to glow in the dark. The paint "charges up" during the daytime when it is light, and that light energy is stored in the paint like a battery. When it goes dark, the paint glows. Alternatively, some glow-in-the-dark paint only works when UV lights are shining on it—that paint is fluorescent, as it wouldn't glow if the UV light was taken away.

CHEMILUMINESCENCE

This is when light is produced by a chemical reaction—for example, glow sticks. The glow stick doesn't need another source of energy to make it glow (like photoluminescent objects do). Instead, two chemicals are mixed, and this mixture gives off light. One of the key chemicals is released when you snap the glow stick, which is why you have to do this essential step to get your sticks to glow.

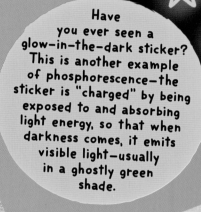

Have you ever seen a glow-in-the-dark sticker? This is another example of phosphorescence—the sticker is "charged" by being exposed to and absorbing light energy, so that when darkness comes, it emits visible light—usually in a ghostly green shade.

Bank of England
TEN Pounds
10
10
E·R

BIOFLUORESCENCE

This is a type of fluorescence found in living organisms. Biofluorescent creatures absorb energy from other sources (for example, the Sun) and then give off light from their body. Biofluorescent creatures include sharks, scorpionfish, flatfish, and wrasses. They swim in shallow water and get energy from the Sun in order to fluoresce. They give off light for many reasons, such as to help them see better, communicate, and attract prey.

Coral is another organism found beneath the sea that can use light to glow. Coral is a marine animal—an invertebrate—and part of the same group as sea anemones. Coral has special pigment in it that glows when the Sun shines on it. For shallow-water coral, this acts as a sunblock, protecting the coral from the UV light that comes from the Sun. Coral that lives deeper in the ocean doesn't need sunblock—so why does it glow? Scientists think it is because the glowing coral creates light for algae that also live deep in the ocean. These algae then produce more oxygen, which in return is good for the coral.

There are many fluorescent fish, and not nearly as many fluorescent animals living on dry land. But there is a polka-dot tree frog that will fluoresce in UV light, although under normal light it looks quite dull! Scientists think that the reason the frog glows in the dark is so that it can communicate with other tree frogs, even at nighttime.

Parrots, budgies, owls, and puffins all have fluorescent colors when you look at them under UV lights. This is interesting because many of these birds can also see in UV light, which they use to find prey or see where their eggs and nests are. Male and female parrots seem identical in visible light but in UV light they look different—so UV light may help parrots find a mate more easily. Owls have fluorescent feathers—and the younger the feathers are, the more they glow in UV light. Puffins have fluorescent beaks, and scientists think this is to help them find a mate. Perhaps that's why the owls glow in the dark, too!

Some butterflies on the African continent have fluorescent scales that change color. They glow blue in the dark after absorbing energy from the Sun.

GO FOR A SPIN

Many types of spiders can also glow in the dark, in a whole range of colors. Scientists still aren't sure why they do this—it could be something that happens when they digest food, for communication, to aid their poor eyesight, to detract from predators, or for reasons we can't even imagine yet.

SEEING IN THE DARK

The darker it is, the less humans are able to see, and as the light dims, we become unable to see color. This is because the cones in our eyes—which let us see colors—don't work very well in the dark.

Rods work better in the dark, but they don't allow us to see colors, so when it gets dark, everything appears to be gray, black, and white. This isn't too much of a problem because generally humans do everything in the daytime, and nowadays we can use flashlights and other lights in the dark to help us see in color.

However, some animals need to be able to see in the dark because that is when they go hunting. These are nocturnal predators, and they include owls, cats, foxes, and tarsiers (nocturnal primates from Asia). These animals can see so well in the dark because they have much bigger eyes than we do, and their eyes have more light-collecting cells, meaning that they have many more rods than cones. Some animals also have a mirrored layer called a tapetum inside their eyes, which reflects the light to make it brighter.

DID YOU KNOW?

Tapetums are the reason why cats' eyes glow!

NIGHT VISION

Elephant hawk moths have exceptional night vision. Their eyes have large lenses, and light doesn't have to travel too far into their eyes to hit the cones and allow them to see color. Evolutionary changes mean the moths can see in ultraviolet, yellow, and blue, even on a really dark night. This helps them find flowers and feed at nighttime. Some small primates, like aye-ayes and lemurs, can also see color in the dark, including blue and some shades of green. Being able to see blue at night means they can see the fruits and seeds of their favorite food source, the palm tree, and they might also be able to feast on the insects that love these fruits. Being able to see green means they can find young, healthy leaves with the most nutritional content. This is handy for when the lemurs need extra food—for example, when they are new parents.

HOW DO BATS SEE IN DARK CAVES?

You might have heard the phrase "blind as a bat," but in reality, bats can see. Most bats can see as well as a human, but in the dark, sight isn't the sense they rely on. Bats have special abilities to be able to navigate in dark caves.

They also "see" the world using sound—with something called echolocation. A bat will screech, click, and squeal—a sound too high-pitched for humans to hear. The sound bounces off cave walls or other objects, and the bats hear the echo and are able to work out how big their cave is, or how far away prey is. These flying mammals can feel infrared light in their noses, so their noses act like heat-seeking sensors.

SEEING RAINBOWS

The mantis shrimp has sixteen special cones in its eyes (humans have just three), and sees ten times more color than the average human. It is believed that this shrimp sees more colors than any other animal on the planet. They see the visible spectrum, UV, and infrared, and each eye is on a separate stalk so they can look in two directions at the same time!

WHAT ABOUT BLACK AND WHITE?

We have talked a lot about the colors of the rainbow, but what about black and white? And why isn't brown in the visible color spectrum?

As we know, white light is made up of all the colors of the rainbow mixed together. If you split white light up, you make a rainbow.

This means that for us to see white, all the colors of the rainbow need to be reflected off an object and into our eyes. If you look at a white T-shirt, it's actually reflecting red, green, violet, and everything in between.

Black is the opposite: the absence of color. We see black because black objects absorb all the colors of the rainbow. As for brown, have you ever mixed red, yellow, and blue paint? If you have, you'll know you get a brown color. The same thing happens with the colors of light. Brown is created when all colors except for red and green are absorbed. Red and green reflected into our eyes mix to make brown. Or, as a scientist would say, on the color spectrum brown is created when the visible colors with long wavelengths (reds, oranges, and yellows) are combined with low luminance (intensity of light) or low saturation.

If a color is highly saturated, it is very bright. If its saturation is low, it looks washed out, tending more toward gray scale.

WHAT COLOR IS A POLAR BEAR UNDER ITS FUR?

As you may know, polar bears are massive white bears that live in the Arctic. They spend their life against a backdrop of snow and ice, so their white fur helps them blend in with their surroundings, and lets them camouflage themselves in snowdrifts so they can find food, such as seals. However, even though polar bears look white, their fur is actually made of hollow, see-through fibers. And underneath, their skin is black.

The reason that polar bears don't look black is because their fur is thick and it reflects visible light. When the Sun is blazing down on them, they look brilliant white because the clear hollow hairs let all the colors of light through. The reason the hair is hollow is so that it can trap extra heat and insulate the bears from the cold. Their skin is black because black absorbs the most light from the Sun and so helps to keep the polar bears warm.

But if a polar bear has eaten a lot of seal oil, their fur becomes tinged yellow—and even more strangely, you might sometimes see a green polar bear. This happens because warmer temperatures means small green algae start to grow in their fur, which affects bears that live in areas impacted by climate change, and those in zoos. Time to put those bears in the bath!

IS A ZEBRA BLACK WITH WHITE STRIPES OR WHITE WITH BLACK STRIPES?

For a long time, scientists didn't know the answer. But recently, we've found out that zebras are in fact black with white stripes.

People used to think that zebras were white with black stripes, partly because on their underbelly and down their legs, the black stripes seem to disappear and there are areas of white. But if you were to shave a zebra, you would see it has black skin underneath the hair.

The stripes are there to help zebras keep away from predators. In a pack, zebra stripes can confuse lions or leopards, who don't know who to chase. The stripes "flicker" when the herd of zebras are running, and this can throw predators off. The stripes stop the zebras from being bitten by flies, as flies don't like to land on striped surfaces. The stripes keep the zebras at a nice temperature, too: not too hot or too cold. The stripes are a form of identification—a bit like our fingerprints, each zebra's pattern is completely individual.

WHY DOES SPACE LOOK BLACK?

Space appears black to the human eye partly because it is so massive. It would take a long time to travel from one object in the universe to another, so even though there is a lot of stuff in the universe, because it is so big it seems empty—and dark.

There are billions of stars in the universe, so you might think that space should be super bright. But space is so huge—and getting bigger all the time—that the light from all those stars takes millions and millions of years to get to us.

In fact, many of the stars in the universe aren't old enough for their light to have reached us yet, so we can't see them at all. And because the universe is getting bigger, the light from all those billions of stars is being stretched, so their wavelengths are getting longer, past the red part of the visible spectrum into wavelengths like infrared that we can't see with our eyes.

A light-year is the measurement of the distance light travels in one year—nearly six trillion miles!

So, ARE there Rainbows in SPACE?

THE COLOR Rainbow

The word *rainbow* comes from a Latin word that means "rainy arch."

RAINBOWS AT A GLANCE

What do you do when you see a rainbow in the sky? I often stop in my tracks, take a photo, make a wish, and leave with a smile on my face. Rainbows are displays of science and nature at their best, and they have different symbolism in religions and cultures around the world.

Ancient people first thought rainbows were made up of three, then four, then five colors. It wasn't until the seventeenth century that the seven-color rainbow was agreed upon in the Western world.

Although we learn the seven visible colors of the rainbow, in reality a rainbow isn't seven bands of color but an arch of many colors blended into each other. Different people and different cultures disagree on different numbers of colors in a rainbow.

There have been stories about the human love of rainbows for thousands of years. They range from Bible stories about Noah, in which God sent a rainbow as a promise that the world wouldn't flood again, to Norse tales of a rainbow that connects the world of humans to the world of the gods, to Australian Aboriginal folklore about a rainbow snake that is the creator of the world.

And you may have heard about the Irish legend of the pot of gold at the end of the rainbow!

HOW DO YOU MAKE A RAINBOW?

Rainbows have interested scientists and philosophers for thousands of years. People like the Greek scholar and thinker Aristotle (384–322 BCE) and the Roman playwright, politician, and philosopher Seneca the Younger (died around 65 CE) mention rainbows in their work, and around the tenth century, Ibn al-Haytham (Alhazen) (965–1039 CE)— an Arab mathematician, astronomer, and physicist—started to try and come up with explanations for them.

A German monk named Theodoric was the first person to document how to make a rainbow. In 1307, he filled a large glass bowl with water and watched what happened when sunlight shone through it. Then he measured the angles of the light.

Isaac Newton (later made famous for his theories of the laws of gravity) showed that white light from the Sun could be split into a rainbow—he counted seven colors—by using a prism.

As we know, the light from the Sun is white light—all the colors of the rainbow mixed together. The water in the glass bowl and the prism causes the light to split up into what looks like the separate colors of the rainbow.

You need three things to see a rainbow: light, a clear liquid or a prism, and a person to view it. This would work with sunlight (light), rain droplets (liquid), and you (a person to view it!). The lower the Sun is in the sky, the bigger and brighter the rainbow appears. So you have the best chance of seeing a rainbow if a rain shower happens around sunset. The rainbow will always form directly opposite the Sun.

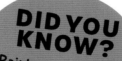

DID YOU KNOW?
Rainbows can be full circles. But we normally see rainbows as arcs because the ground gets in the way!

SEEING DOUBLE

Double rainbows are formed when the light from the Sun reflects twice inside the water droplets. In this case, the first rainbow starts with red on the outside and finishes with violet on the inside, and the second rainbow starts with violet and finishes with red on the inside. This is all because of the way that light is bent and reflected by the water in the rain.

You can't actually get close to a rainbow. Rainbows are created because of the way that the light and the liquid interact with each other, so rainbows aren't physical objects that you can walk up to and touch.

Did you know that there are also moonbows? These are rainbows created by the light from the Moon (reflected light from the Sun) instead of direct light from the Sun.

WHAT DO RAINBOWS REPRESENT?

What does seeing a rainbow mean to you? Often, they are seen as a symbol of hope and happiness, and because they are common after a storm, sometimes people see them as a sign of better times to come. Rainbows can be seen as a sign of good luck, because of the pot of gold said to be at the end of them.

RAINBOW FLAGS

Rainbow flags have been used for many years to represent cooperation and togetherness, such as during the German Peasants' War (1524–1525). It has also been the universal symbol of pride for the LGBTQ+ community since the 1970s.

In 1978, an openly gay man and drag queen, Gilbert Baker, created the rainbow flag as a symbol of pride for his community.

DID YOU KNOW?

The highest-rated rainbow-related song is a cover version of "Somewhere Over the Rainbow" sung by Israel Kamakawiwo'ole—it has had more than one billion views on YouTube.

FUN FACT

The record for the longest-lasting rainbow was six hours—recorded over Wetherby in Yorkshire, England, from 9 a.m. until 3 p.m. on March 14, 1994. But that was beaten by a rainbow in Yangmingshan, a national park near Taipei, on November 30, 2017. That one lasted for a whopping eight hours and fifty-eight minutes!

RAINBOW FAMILY

People might refer to a family unit as a "rainbow family." This could refer to a family that includes LGBTQ+ members, or a family with same-sex parents.

NHS

The National Health Service (NHS) is the United Kingdom's public-health service. During the COVID-19 pandemic, the rainbow became a symbol to celebrate the NHS and the key workers who supported the general public.

ARE there RAINBOWS in SPACE?

Wherever you have drops of water and a light source, you can make a rainbow. To make a rainbow on Earth you can use sunshine and water droplets. The sunlight shines through raindrops, which split the white sunlight into its rainbow of colors. But the water droplets don't have to be rain—you can make your own rainbows with a hose or water gun, and you can sometimes see rainbows at a fountain.

To get a rainbow in space you would also need light and liquid, but it doesn't have to be sunlight—and it doesn't have to be water! Any type of liquid would also split the white light into its rainbow colors, although a rainbow made from another liquid might look a bit different from a water rainbow. What do you think a space rainbow would look like?

There aren't many places in space that we know of that have liquid water in enough quantities to create rain and raindrops—but there is a moon of Saturn called Titan, which has rivers, lakes, and streams, just like Earth. But the liquid isn't water, it is liquid methane—which we see on Earth in a gas form. In fact, methane gas on Earth often comes from living creatures, like cows, when they pass wind!

On Titan the conditions are different, and methane exists in its liquid form. There is a cycle on Titan just like the water cycle, but it is called the methane cycle. So because Titan has liquid oceans and rain, and gets light from the Sun, rainbows could be made on that moon. Titan has a thick atmosphere, though, so direct sunlight is less common, and there is less chance of a rainbow forming.

IMAGINING A SPACE RAINBOW

As far as we know, there is nothing living on Titan to observe these potential rainbows, and we haven't managed to photograph any yet from a space probe. But if we were able to observe space rainbows, we can imagine they would be wider and broader than the ones we see on Earth because of the methane, but be made up of the same colors—red on the outside, orangey in the middle, and violet on the inside.

VENUS GLORY

Another type of rainbow you might find in space would be something called a Venus glory. This has actually been observed by the spacecraft *Venus Express*. Glories aren't arcs of color like rainbows, but instead they are smaller concentric circles with a bright center, a bit like a bull's-eye. They are formed in a different way to rainbows, too.

On Venus there are lots of droplets of sulfuric acid in the atmosphere. These droplets are able to mix with the light from the Sun, causing us to see rings of color. The *Venus Express* spacecraft positioned itself in between the clouds and the Sun in order to spot the glories, and it did!

We are always finding more planets and moons outside our own solar system, and it is also possible that these planets, called exoplanets, might have the right conditions to form other rainbows in space, too.

The universe is an incredible place—and there is so much more to see. Who knows what we will discover next?

Liquid methane refracts (bends) the light in a different way from water. This is what would give the rainbow its wider shape.

We can observe glories on Earth, too—so make sure you look out for them the next time you go in an airplane or go hiking up a foggy mountain.

119

GLOSSARY

ALBINISM, ALBINO
Albinism is a condition in which a person or an animal is born without natural pigment, or color, in their skin, hair, and eyes. When a person or animal has albinism, their skin and hair will be white, and their eyes are usually pink.

ANTHOCYANIN
Anthocyanin is the name of a red pigment, or color, found in plants. It is found in strawberries and helps color plants such as violets and purple carrots, for example.

ASTEROID COLLISIONS
Asteroids are small pieces of rock that orbit the Sun. Scientists think they are made of material left over when the solar system formed. Pieces of asteroid rock can collide with Earth. Sometimes asteroid rock contains gold.

AURORA BOREALIS, AURORA AUSTRALIS
The Sun releases energy particles into space all the time. This energy is known as the solar wind. When the solar wind hits particles of gas in the Earth's atmosphere, it heats them up and they glow and ripple. We can see the glowing gases at night—oxygen glows green, and nitrogen glows a purple-blue color. "Aurora" is the name given to the glowing gases. Aurora borealis, the northern lights, can be seen in northern countries, and Aurora australis, the southern lights, can be seen in southern countries. Spacecraft have also seen auroras on Mars, Jupiter, and Saturn.

BETA-CAROTENE
Beta-carotene is the name of an orange pigment, or color, found in plants. It is beta-carotene that gives orange carrots their color. When humans eat plants containing this pigment, it turns into vitamin A, which helps us to see and keep healthy.

BIOFLUORESCENCE
Biofluorescence is a kind of light that occurs naturally in living things. A biofluorescent creature can absorb light from a source like the Sun, then give out light from its own body. There are biofluorescent varieties of sharks and coral.

BIOLUMINESCENCE
Bioluminescence describes light that comes from a living thing. Light is made by mixing chemicals in the body. A glowworm—the larva of a firefly—makes light to show a possible predator that it isn't good to eat. An angler fish can light part of its body to attract prey.

CALCIUM CARBONATE
Calcium carbonate is a compound, or mixture, of the element calcium and carbonate ions. The carbonate ion is a group of atoms with an electrical charge made up of one carbon atom and three oxygen atoms.

CAROTENEMIA
Carotenemia is a medical condition in which your skin turns yellowy-orange because you have eaten too many vegetables, such as carrots, containing the pigment carotene! If you stop eating the vegetables, your skin will gradually return to its normal color.

CHLOROPHYLL
Chlorophyll is a green pigment, or color, found in plants. Chlorophyll helps a plant make food by taking energy from the Sun. Together with water and carbon dioxide, the plant makes sap. In autumn and winter, when there is less sun, the green in leaves can fade completely, and the leaves look red, yellow, or brown.

COMBUSTION

Combustion is a chemical reaction that takes place between oxygen and a fuel, such as gas or wood. Heat from friction, such as a match being struck, causes the oxygen and fuel to combust. They burn, giving off heat and light in the form of flames.

COMPLEMENTARY COLOR

A color wheel is a way of showing how colors relate to each other by arranging them in a circle. A complementary color is the color directly opposite any color in the wheel.

CORAL BLEACHING

Ultraviolet light from the Sun makes coral turn white. This is known as coral bleaching. The heat makes the coral get rid of algae that live in its tissues and give it color. The coral is not dead, but it is stressed, which is not good for it.

DEFLECT

To turn aside, or make something else turn aside. Red light travels in long wavelengths, and can pass through your skin. Blue light travels in short wavelengths, which are deflected, or bounced back, off your skin. You can see the reflected blue light, which is why veins can look blue.

DISPERSE

To scatter something over a wide area. White light can be dispersed using a prism—it breaks up into the colors of the rainbow.

DOMESTICATION

Domestication is a process in which humans deliberately change wild plants or animals to make them more useful for people.

ECHOLOCATION

Echolocation is a way of finding out where an object is by directing a sound at it, and measuring how long it takes for the echo to come back. Bats use echolocation to help them fly in the dark.

EMIT

To send something out—a sound, a smell, or a light. The Sun emits light, for example.

EVOLVE, EVOLUTION

A process of change in plants or animals that takes place over a long period of time. Dogs have evolved to be color-blind, because this helps them see better in the dark.

EXOPLANETS

An exoplanet is a planet orbiting a star outside our solar system. The first exoplanet officially recognized was in 1992.

EXOSKELETON

An exoskeleton is a supporting structure outside the body of an animal. Crabs have exoskeletons, and so do corals.

FILAMENT

A thin wire, thread, or stalk. In a flower, a filament is the stalk of a stamen. An angler fish has a filament on its head with a ball on the end, which the fish can light up to attract prey.

FLUORESCENCE

Fluorescence is the ability of an object to give off its own light. It is able to absorb short wavelengths of light, then give out longer wavelengths of light. Some glow-in-the-dark paint is fluorescent.

GENETIC MUTATION

Genetic mutation is an unusual change in the DNA of a living thing. When humans tried to grow sweeter carrots, they found the color changed from purple to orange! That was a genetic mutation.

GIBBOUS

Gibbous describes the shape of the Moon when the illuminated part is bigger than a semicircle and smaller than a whole circle. *Gibbous* comes from the Latin word for a hump.

GRAY SCALE
Shades of gray ranging from white to black.

HEMATITE
Hematite is a mineral that contains iron, and is a reddish-brown color. It has been used to make a reddish-purple pigment. Hematite is one of the oldest pigments known, and has been used all over the world.

IRIDESCENCE
Iridescence describes being able to see different colors in one object when it's looked at from different angles. Soap bubbles are iridescent.

ISCHIAL CALLOSITIES
Ischial callosities describe the colored bottoms of some monkeys. *Ischial* is a word for the area at the base of the spine, and *callosities* describes the skin—these monkeys don't have fur on their rear ends.

LARVAE
Larvae are the immature forms of insects. A caterpillar is the larva of a butterfly or moth.

LUMINANCE
Luminance describes the strength of light emitted from a surface in a particular direction.

LUMINESCENCE
Luminescence is light given off by an object that hasn't been heated. Fireflies and their larvae glowworms are luminescent.

MAGENTA
Magenta is a purple-red color. The name was given to a dye first made in 1859: It is the name of a place in northern Italy where a battle between France and Austria was fought in that year.

MAGNETIC FIELD
A magnetic field is the area around a magnet in which its power to attract can be felt. The Earth is a magnet, and has a magnetic field that protects us from the solar wind.

MALLEABLE, MALLEABILITY
A material, such as metal, that can be pressed or hammered into a shape without breaking is described as malleable.

MANGANESE
Manganese is a hard gray metal element. It has been used to make a purple pigment, and is one of the oldest pigments known.

METHANE
On Earth, methane is a colorless gas that has no smell. It can burn, and is the main ingredient of natural gas. Much of Earth's methane comes from living things, such as cows when they pass wind. On Titan, one of Saturn's moons, it is cold enough for methane to be found in liquid form.

MICROBIOLOGY
Microbiology is the study of tiny organisms, such as viruses and bacteria, using microscopes.

MONOCHROME
A picture made in only one color. Black-and-white photos are monochrome.

NOCTURNAL
Nocturnal describes events and activities that happen at night. Many animals are nocturnal.

OPTICAL ILLUSION
An optical illusion is an image that tricks your eye into seeing something that isn't there. Veins can look blue, but our blood is red! The blue color comes from blue light bouncing off your skin into your eyes.

PHOSPHORESCENCE
Phosphorescence is light that can be given out by an object without any source of active energy. Glow-in-the-dark paint can absorb light energy, then release it for some time after the light source has gone.

PHOSPHORS

Phosphors are chemicals that can absorb light, then release it. Phosphors are what make some paint phosphorescent.

PHOTOLUMINESCENCE

Photoluminescence describes the ability of an object to absorb light from a separate source, then release it. Fluorescence and phosphorescence are both forms of photoluminescence.

PHYTOPLANKTON

Plankton are very small organisms—plants and animals—that drift on the surface of the sea. Phytoplankton are the tiniest kinds of plankton.

PIGMENT

A pigment is a color. It can be the natural color of an animal or a plant, or a substance, usually inorganic and in powder form, that can be used to make paint or ink. Pigments are almost always insoluble in water.

PORPHYROPHOBIA

Porphyrophobia is the scientific name for the fear of the color purple.

PRISM

A transparent block, usually with three rectangular sides and triangular ends. When white light is passed through a prism, it splits into separate colors like a rainbow.

RAYLEIGH SCATTERING

When sunlight hits molecules in the Earth's atmosphere, the different wavelengths of light are scattered about. Blue light comes in short, small waves, and is scattered about the most. This is why we see a blue sky in daytime. Lord Rayleigh, who discovered this, was a British scientist in the nineteenth century.

RETINA

A retina is part of the eye. Light goes through the pupil of an eye, and reaches the retina, at the back. The retina is made up of light-sensitive cells, named rods and cones.

RODS AND CONES

Rods and cones are the names of cells found in the retina. Rods detect light and dark, so are sensitive to black and white. Cones detect bright light and colors. Humans have three cones in their eye. The mantis shrimp has sixteen!

SATURATION

Saturation describes how much light is present when you look at a colored object. High saturation means there is plenty of light and the color is bright. Low saturation means the light is dim, and the color looks dull and washed out.

STRUCTURAL COLORIZATION

Structural colorization is an optical illusion! Very thin films on the surface of something can reflect different wavelengths of light. Our eyes see the color of the reflected light rather than the actual color underneath. A peacock's tail feathers are brown, but we see the reflected blues and greens. Different amounts of pigment in the iris of an eye produce a range of colors that depend on how we see the light reflected. Blue light isn't absorbed at all—we see blue eyes because all the wavelengths of blue light are reflected back.

SYNESTHESIA

Synesthesia is a rare condition in which one sense takes on the characteristics of another sense. People with synesthesia might be able to "hear" color or "see" sound.

TAPETUM

A tapetum is a mirror layer in the eyes of some nocturnal animals, which reflects light and helps them see at night. Their eyes shine in the dark, like a cat's.

VISIBLE SPECTRUM

The visible spectrum is the light we can see. Visible light is part of electromagnetic radiation, waves of energy connected with electric and magnetic fields that radiate through space. Infrared, ultraviolet, and X-rays are all part of electromagnetic radiation. The visible spectrum contains wavelengths of all the colors of the rainbow. Some animals can see in areas beyond the visible spectrum.

ACKNOWLEDGMENTS

Thank you to the rainbow key workers who kept us safe and the country running during the coronavirus pandemic. Particularly the Ks and Fs who worked tirelessly at the front line, the teachers who never stopped, and to those who lost their lives and loved ones. We are eternally grateful.